DEADLY ANIMALS

By **MARTHA HOLMES**
Illustrated by **MIKE VAUGHAN**

ATHENEUM 1991 NEW YORK
COLLIER MACMILLAN CANADA · TORONTO

Thresher Shark

Out of the blue comes the thresher shark. He has seen a school of small fish. With a swirl of his long tail he sweeps past them, herding them closer together. Around and around he swims, in ever smaller circles, until the fish are in a tight ball. Suddenly he turns and rushes straight at them with his mouth wide open.

Dart Poison Frog

The dart poison frog is beautifully colored, but anything that eats it will die. Its skin produces one of the most deadly poisons in the world. South American Indians use only the tiniest amount of the poison on their blow-darts when they hunt for food in the forest.

King Cobra

The king cobra lies coiled, guarding her eggs in a rough nest of twigs. She hears men shouting and soon sees the huge trunk of an elephant. She stands high and hisses violently. Her head shoots forward and she bites the elephant's trunk, injecting a deadly poison through her two large fangs. In half an hour the elephant is dead.

Harpy Eagle

Perched high in the rain forest is the harpy eagle, one of the largest of all birds of prey. It glides down off its perch and with short broad wings soars through the dense forest with ease. The eagle spots a monkey. It turns and swoops down, reaching 50 mph, and snatches it from the branches. The monkey is as big as the eagle, but is easily lifted up into the forest **canopy**, where the eagle will feed.

Spotted Hyena

Slinking through the scrub at dusk the hyena lets out a peculiar howl that starts hoarse and low and ends up a high-pitched yelp. Gazelles freeze as they are, and listen. The hyena is joined by others and they trot off toward the nervous herd. Most of the gazelles speed away, but one old buck struggles to keep up. Within seconds the hyenas have grabbed him by the legs, pulled him down, and started eating him alive. Now the hunt is over, and their blood-curdling 'giggling' sounds across the African night.

Killer Whale

The attack is carefully timed. Riding the waves, the killer whale races toward the land and is thrown up onto the shore. Its jaws open and grab a startled sea lion. Then, with huge effort, it turns and heaves itself back down the beach until another wave crashes down and it is carried back out to sea.

Cheetah

Well hidden in long dry grass, the cheetah has stalked the herd of grazing gazelle. Suddenly he bounds out and the chase is on. He selects a young one and in three seconds is traveling at 70 mph. He is the fastest runner in the animal world, and the **fawn** cannot get away. Running at full speed, the cheetah trips it with his paw and pounces, panting but triumphant.

Hippopotamus

Hippos spend their day resting in rivers or lakes, and that's where they are happiest. At night they climb out to go and feed on grass. A man walking by the edge of the river in the early morning doesn't know he is crossing the hippo's escape route. At the sound of footsteps the hippo turns and runs fast back toward the water. Suddenly he comes across the man and in his fright becomes very fierce. His jaws open wide and then close on the man, biting him in half. People in the **bush** fear hippos as much as lions, and with good reason.

Electric Eel

In the murky Amazon river the electric eel cannot see very much, so it sends out tiny electric waves which bounce back to it from the small fish nearby. The eel's special **electroreceptors**, dotted along its body, understand the returned signal: there is something worth eating ahead. Zap! The eel stuns the fish with an electric shock, then gulps it down. This shock is strong enough to knock out a man.

Red Piranha

Toward the end of the dry season, when the rivers are low, they are found together in great numbers. A boy driving his herd of cattle across the river doesn't realize the danger. The hungry fish smell the blood seeping from a recent wound on the cow's legs and dart toward her. She stumbles as they bite her legs, then more and more fish attack. Their feeding frenzy lasts only a few minutes. The cow has been completely eaten.

Indian Tiger

The tiger is a killing machine of enormous power. In the falling dusk he is silently stalking a buffalo from downwind. As soon as he is within 4 yards of his victim he will spring forward with one huge bound, claws outstretched, and land on the victim's neck. With a bite of the tiger's powerful jaws the buffalo is dead in less than a minute. The tiger drags its prey away to a deep, dark place in the jungle. There's enough food here for 2 days' feasting.

Thresher Shark
Fish

Length: 20 ft. **Weight:** 990 lbs.

Home:
Found in all oceans between 30 and 100 yards deep.

Food:
Mackerel, herring, pilchard, and squid.

Family Life:
Live alone except when mating. Gives birth to 2–6 fully formed pups of up to 1.5 yards. That's a bit longer than a bicycle.

Superpower:
Its huge tail. Can jump 5.5 yards clear of water.

Did You Know?
Some people have mistaken it for a dinosaur like the Loch Ness Monster in Scotland. When its long tail is sticking out of the water it looks like the monster's curved neck.

Enemies:
Man.

Dart Poison Frogs
Amphibian

Length: 1.5 ins. **Weight:** ⅓ oz.

Home:
Found in South America in tropical rain forests.

Food:
Very small insects and ants.

Family Life:
About 10 eggs are produced and guarded by the male. When the tadpoles hatch they wriggle onto his back and he carries them to a good feeding ground. They probably live for 2–3 years.

Superpower:
Poison. A speck of poison smaller than a grain of salt is enough to kill a person.

Did You Know?
Indians catch the frogs, extract the poison, dip their darts in it, and then go hunting. One frog can produce enough poison for 40 darts.

Enemies:
Man's destruction of their forests.

King Cobra
Reptile

Length: 13 ft., but the record is 18 ft. That's as long as a giraffe. **Weight:** 6 lbs.

Home:
Forests and farms in India and Southeast Asia.

Food:
Snakes, rats, lizards, and birds.

Family Life:
The female and male dance in front of each other before mating. She lays about 20 eggs and is the only snake to build a nest. Cobras live for about 8 years.

Superpower:
Poison. If not treated, a man would die within 20 minutes of being bitten.

Did You Know?
A cobra uses its forked tongue to "smell" the air. It picks up the scent and carries it back to a "tasting" spot on the roof of its mouth.

Enemies:
Men kill cobras for their skins.

Harpy Eagle
Bird of prey

Height: 3 ft. **Weight:** female is heavier than the male and reaches weights of 20 lbs.

Home:
Forests in southern Mexico, eastern Bolivia, and Argentina.

Food:
Monkeys, sloths, and tree porcupines.

Family Life:
A pair of eagles mate for life. They build a big nest about 10 feet long at the top of a tree, as high as 160 feet. As far as we know they only have one egg every other year.

Superpower:
Speed and strength. It can fly straight upward. Few if any other birds can do that.

Did You Know?
It has the most powerful feet of any bird of prey.

Enemies:
It is threatened only by man's destruction of its jungles.

Spotted Hyena
Mammal

Length: 5 ft. **Height:** 30 ins. **Weight:** between 110 and 175 lbs.

Home:
Dry open grasslands and bush in many parts of Africa.

Food:
Eats almost anything alive or dead, from zebras to campfire rubbish.

Family Life:
They hunt and **scavenge** alone or in packs. Normally have 3 cubs which are looked after by the mother in a shared den. They live for about 25 years.

Superpower:
Teeth. Its front teeth are 1.5 inches long and can strip flesh from bones. The molars or back teeth then grind the bones down to a fine powder.

Did You Know?
It has a **digestive** system that can absorb almost anything.

Enemies:
Cubs are easy **prey** to many animals including male hyenas.

Killer Whale
Mammal

Length: 22 ft. but can grow as long as 35 ft. **Weight:** as much as 9,900 lbs. That's as heavy as 60 people.

Home:
All oceans.

Food:
Small whales, squid, dolphins, seals, and fish.

Family Life:
Live in groups called "pods" with one male plus a **harem** of 3–39 females. Pregnancy lasts 15 months and the babies are yellow and black. They can live up to 100 years.

Superpower:
Hunting in well-organized groups. They can stay underwater for 20 minutes, dive as deep as 1,000 yards, and leap into the air as far as 40 feet.

Did You Know?
Killer whales are dangerous in the sea, but can be trained to perform tricks in zoos.

Enemies:
Man.

Cheetah
Mammal

 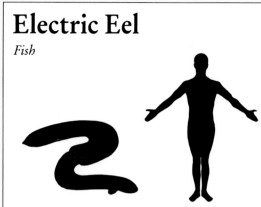

Length: 7.5 ft. **Height:** 3 ft.
Weight: 55 lbs.

Home:
Mainly on open plains in eastern Africa.

Food:
Gazelle, often bigger than itself.

Family Life:
Normally live alone. The female has about 3 cubs at a time and she carries them to a new hiding place every few days. The father takes no part in looking after the babies. Live up to 12 years.

Superpower:
Streamlined speed. It has a very flexible bone structure which helps it take extralong strides.

Did You Know:
Mothers give their cubs hunting lessons by bringing back live **prey** and releasing it for them to chase.

Enemies:
Adult cheetahs can outrun anything, but cubs can be taken by hyenas, lions, and wild dogs.

Hippopotamus
Mammal

Length: 11 ft. **Height:** 5 ft.
Weight: 3,000–7,000 lbs. That's as much as 2 small cars.

Home:
Freshwater lakes and rivers in Africa.

Food:
Graze at night on grass.

Family Life:
Live alone or in groups of mothers and babies or in gangs of males. Males guard their patch by throwing water, grunting loudly, and stretching their mouths as wide as possible to scare off other males. They live for about 45 years.

Superpower:
Jaws. They can open them as wide as 150° and could bite you in half.

Did You Know?
Terrapins and young crocodiles bask on the backs of hippos.

Enemies:
Lions and crocodiles attack young hippos.

Electric Eel
Fish

Length: 7.5 ft. **Weight:** 60 lbs.

Home:
Rivers in South America.

Food:
Small fish.

Family Life:
When levels of water change during the rainy season the female knows it's time to breed. The female lays her eggs after a **courtship display**. Length of life is not known.

Superpower:
Electric charge. Has 3 electric organs. It produces electricity at 200–300 volts, which can badly shock a man. The charge is strong enough to switch on 300 radios.

Did You Know?
Fish are the only animals that can make electricity. The only mammal able to detect electricity is the duckbilled platypus.

Enemies:
None.

Red Piranha

Fish

Length: 16 ins. **Weight:** 4.4 lbs.

Home:
Found in deep rivers in Central and South America.

Food:
Wounded and diseased fish.

Family Life:
When rivers become low and food is scarce, large **shoals** of piranhas get together and attack much larger animals. The female lays eggs during the yearly floods and keeps watch over them once they have hatched.

Superpower:
Teeth. So sharp they can devour a cow in a few minutes, leaving only a skeleton. Infrared eyesight. To see through the muddy river water.

Did You Know?
Piranhas only attack large animals that are wounded or already dead.

Enemies:
Man catches them to eat.

Indian Tiger

Mammal

Length: 9 ft. **Height:** 3 ft. **Weight:** 495 lbs. That's as heavy as 3 men.

Home:
Lives in jungles or thick **bush** in India.

Food:
Deer, buffalo, and wild pig.

Family Life:
Normally live and hunt alone. They are fiercely **territorial**. Home ground is constantly marked by spraying urine and by scratching trees and the ground with its claws. Females have about 3 to 5 cubs at a time. The mother brings them up in a "**den**." Live for up to 15 years.

Superpower:
Incredibly strong. Its dark stripes meld it into the background as it creeps stealthily through the forest on velvet paws.

Did You Know?
Tigers love going swimming. A mother teaches her cubs to swim by pulling them in.

Enemies:
Man.

Glossary

Amphibian: Breathes air. Has moist, smooth skin. Lays eggs in water.

Breed: Having babies.

Bush: Area covered by patchy undergrowth and plants.

Canopy: Leafy top part of trees or forest.

Courtship display: Showing off to attract the female.

Den: A home either in a cave or under a bush.

Digestive system: Stomach and intestines.

Electroreceptors: Areas for receiving electric messages.

Fawn: Young gazelle.

Harem: Group of females.

Mammal: Breathes air. Gives birth to live young and feeds them on milk.

Predator: An animal that hunts or eats other animals.

Prey: An animal taken by a predator for food.

Reptile: Breathes air. Lays soft- shelled eggs. Has scaly skin.

Scavenge: To look for and eat rubbish.

Shoal: Large group of fish.

Terrapin: A small tortoiselike animal that lives in fresh water.

Territorial: Guards home ground where the animal hunts and lives.

Measurements are based on average adult sizes.